UNSENT LETTERS

"SOULFULLY YOURS"

PRACHE ARSHI

"TO UNCONDITIONAL LOVE"

AND

TO ALL THOSE WHO DARE

TO LOVE UNCONDITIONALLY.

Contents

Contents

Contents

Contents

Contents

1. Graffiti

The graffiti on the walls of my heart
have some vague images
of our togetherness from some distant past.
I don't recogonise you as such.
You are not from my gene pool
neither are you from my blood chain...
but somehow you work as an antedote
to all my stress and pain!
Looks like there's some magnet in you
for I helplessly give in to your mystical pull!
I have never met you in person
but I wish to embody your essence,
so that before doubts creap in
and before some hopeless thoughts seep in...
I want to engrave all our unsaid tales,
like how lovers inscribe their names
on an old Oak tree.

2. Stop it

When I stopped asking for your help,
you provided me all that I needed.
When I stopped sharing my thoughts,
you read them all aloud.
When I stopped solving the puzzle,
you revealed the missing pieces in my blurry vision.
When I stopped looking for you,
you started showing up everywhere.
Please stop playing this unfathomable game,
what I seek is just your love again!

3. Guardian Angel

Are you an Angel,
that is often glorified in the childhood stories
or a Devil
who comes in disguise to cast a dreadful shadow.
You play with me,
do things that brings me a smile making me feel alive!
Your warmth is more genuine then the wrath that you display.
Sometimes I get swayed,
fooled by your cunning ways.
But then there's a flash and everthing becomes crystal clear.
Now I know
you are not two people but one and its all just a role play.

4. Conversations

Of all the wordly pleasures
I will always choose
late night soulful conversations with you
under the starlit sky...

5. First love

A realisation has settled deep in my heart
it's in perfect sync with the eternal love stories ever told.
I stand still to soak in this bliss,
it's surreal and yet so real.
It feels as if I'm teleported to
a magical World...
where my wishes get instantly fulfilled!
And sometimes it looks like a mirage,
where my hungry soul wanders in the sweltering heat
in search of loving warmth!
The impression keeps changing
in the mirror of my heart,
as days and nights pass.
So I hold myself tight in the dark
to stay calm without disturbing the wind
and believe in the placating stories of my
heart which say that...
"You will always be,
my first love and last hope,
You will always be mine!!!"
I'm happy and at peace
in this state of hope and desire.

6. Realisation

Realisation has dawned upon perhaps too late
it's not a game of pefect time and place,
but of luck and fate.
Realisation has dawned upon perhaps too late
it's not a game of love and hate,
but of give and take.
Realisation has dawned upon perhaps too late
it's not a game of me and you
but of falsity and truth!

7. Wildfire

I covered distances beyond measure,
came across some wonderful souls but there
remained an unfulfilled desire.
A subtle but very persistent,
like the constant flow of the blood in my viens.
A desire to feel complete.
I often used to wonder was I really incomplete?
Multiple times I tried to contemplate and deal with it
with profound logical lies.
Everytime my heart lost the battle to my brain.
Everytime I tried to crush and burn the desire
it turned out to be a wild fire.
I surrendered and learned to live with the unrest
and accepted it whole heartedly
as an answer to my unquenched quest.
Piece by piece my mind shredded my heart and sealed all doors
where the desire used to come and knock.
In that state I lost all hope and then without a knock,
without a ring you walked in unlocking all
the closed doors.
You swept me off my feet making me forever
complete.

8. Underplay

Sometimes to save someone's name,
sometimes to placate someone's ego,
shattered my feelings I was put in my place.
I'm so done with this ongoing underplay.
Either stick by my side and sway
or completely choose to walk away.
Just know this that this time
I have made up my mind
no more I'm going to ever underplay.

9. Unsent Letter

I wish it was as simple as a scrabble game
rearranging letters to form a word.
Ah! These 'unsent letters' are not merely words
these have taken a lot from my being, my soul!
Strewn with fragments of my beating heart,
jagged emotions sharp as a dart!
These are very very fragile
with tender nerves trying hard
to hold potent love that's alive!
Handle with care as I hand them to you
because these are not just some
gibbrish scribbled that wish to kept
in the bookshelf close to you,
but have a soul...
longing to get a reply from you.

10. Walk on the Path

Some walk on the path
following the breadcrumbs.
I walk on the path
following the tea cups.
Some master to run on the path
as if a cakewalk.
I chose to walk
on the razorblade barefoot.
No matter what you follow
as long as you walk...
all paths eventually take you to a place
where you belong!

11. Being

Sun is not burning,
it's just simply being itself.
Moon doesn't have phases,
it's just your perspective.
Earth is not grounded,
you are the one who needs it's pull.
Trees are not just standing still,
they witness the era's pass by.
Rivers don't meander down,
water needs to reach it's destination...
and so is the calling of the soul,
to become one with the whole.

12. One with You

When I disappear,
You appear...
When I dissolve,
You evolve...
When I submerge,
You emerge...
But when there's no I or You
It's difficult to say,
it's Sun or a Moon...
When there's no I or You
It's difficult to say,
the glass is empty or full...
When there's is no I or You
It's difficult to say,
it's real or ... virtual!

13. Ecstasy

Like some cosmic prophecy...
An unheard silent frequency...
Enchanted by your currency...
My soul whirls in ecstasy!

14. Make up your mind

You snatched my every reason of peace
...then sent the beings serenading tranquillity.
You twisted and ripped me apart
then sent angels to heal my wounded heart.
God what are you really up to
please make up your mind!
Getting tired of being strong,
getting killed in this grind
I am starting to get disillusioned,
Show mercy, some love and be little more kind.

15. Who am I?

Who am I?
A story
A riddle
A mystery
A dream
A query
A perception
Or
BEYOND these...
An assumption
An anthology
An existence
An esoteric
An imagination
An answer
Who knows...
Only one thing is certain
that I am everything
and
NOTHING at all!!!

16. Voyage within

The World stirred me up and saw,
just dust particles in me!
I looked at self and realised
Stardust is all that is me!
Thought I will master the self
and seek the sparkling light.
But such is life while on this voyage within,
the self starts to melt away …
The One you are looking for
takes the centre stage
and you become nothing but a spectator.

17. I don't doubt

I don't doubt your presence...
because
I don't question your absence anymore...
I don't doubt your eternal love...
because
I know the hate has turned into affection...
I don't doubt your intentions...
because
I realise you are the purest dimension...

18. The Invisible Path

Sometimes On the path...
Sometimes Off the path...
One breath at a time...
One step at a time...
One day at a time...
Determined to make you mine...

19. Home

HOME is
where the HEART is...
HEART is
where the HOPE is...
HOPE is
where the LIGHT is...
LIGHT is
where the LOVE is...
LOVE is
where the HOME is!

20. No Longer

I'm no longer the seeker,
but the sought...
I'm no longer the dreamer,
but the dream...
I'm no longer the chaser,
but the chosen...
because I'm no longer,
running away from myself!

21. Wonder

The temptations have got definition...
The callings have recieved meaning...
The longings have found their destination...
The hunger has changed the name...
The perseverance has become a means to reach you...
And I still wonder if it's love or...
merely an infatuation!

22. Worth it

The only treasures worth accumulating are,
"Treasures of the Heart"
The only thoughts worth considering are,
"Mindful Thoughts"
The only relation worth maintaining is,
"Relation with the self"
The only love worth falling for is,
"Unconditional Love"
The only pursuit worth the effort is,
"Pursuit of the Divine"

23. Soak in

Soak in the magnificent reality of your being...
You are one of the finest creations of Almighty...
It's an absolute privilege to be born as a
Human being...

24. Story line

With dramatic twists and mind boggling turns
you have made my life no less then a thriller.
With intermittent showers of blessings and love
you have made my life in a way, fairy tale as well!
Getting so used to this roller coaster ride
seems soon enough I will get pro at this play.
But when the pace slows down
I get bored of your storytelling.
The screenplay is crisp
but the narrative sucks sometimes!
Focus on me more O God, add some spice.
I know I'm your favourite character
and you are a MASTER STORYTELLER.

25. Dreams

Some dreams you seamlessly weave...
Some dreams are woven for you...
Some dreams don't let you sleep...
Some dreams don't let you wake up!

26. Desire

In all the things I ever desired,
you were never on my priority list
and
the intensity of my love is such that
now all my lists
begin and end with
YOU.

27. You

You trenched the borders of my heart...
Wrenched my desires without a mark...
Quenched my thirst with your compassion...
Leaving me drenched in your devotion...

28. Nothing

I sweat and sleep
I weep and sweep
I breathe and bleed
I dream and weave
I tred and treat
And
I am NOTHING
but a mere reflection of You Almighty...

29. Letter from you

Still waiting...

30. Heat is on

Sometimes I feel you are brewing me,
to taste like your favourite coffee.
Sometimes I feel you are frying me on simmer,
to be perfectly cooked.
Sometimes I feel you are baking me in an oven,
to satiate your sweet tooth.
Sometimes I even feel you have forgotten,
to turn off the heat.
But at all times...
I know I will turn out to be just perfect
the way you want me to be!

31. Desirable

Okay, I was never deserving enough
to steal a desirable glace from you.
It's a promise I am making to myself,
that one day
you won't be able to
take your eyes off me...
And at that time there won't be apathy,
Desire will be met by Desire indeed!

32. Cocktail

I keep juggling between the chores like a bartender,
just to make sure that I deliver everything
on the table all that is asked of...
I have exausted my entire being in providing the best
but you still get displeased at drop of a hat!
It's dishearting to see a frown in place of a smile on your face!
I do all this only out of pure love and affection.
Stop treating me like your regular cup of tea or a mocktail
for I'm neither of the two.
In me is a bit naughty bit exuberant girl,
a cocktail just like the long island ice tea.
My love for you and your love for me pulls me back,
but in this process I have started losing myself.
Can't you save me from this hopelessness
and just be with me unconditionally?
With full integrity forever, I promise to treat you well.
In return you take a vow not to upend my being ...
because I don't afford to ever again lose myself!

33. Wean off

This is not a request asking for another chance
but a declaration that I have failed
in my numerous attempts to wean off myself
from my addiction of loving you.
So you better show redamancy and accept
me as your Queen.
As enough and more time has already gone by,
just keep your ego aside and say that I belong to you...
and you to me!
Stop being stubborn and please give in my King,
for I can't wean off myself from my addiction of loving you!

34. Secret retreat

There was a place where I dwelled
a cozy little house where everything
belonged to me.
It held me in it's warm embrace
without any despair.
It nurtured me with love and care,
there were no seasons...
no reasons to stress or fear.
All was so bright and beautiful
in my mother's womb.
Battling my way through nights and days
battered and bruised handling wordly affairs.
Tried best to get some hope some peace
but never could I get that sound sleep.
Then one day I got so tired that I fell...
looked up at heavens and surrenderd myself!
In that moment time stood still
and I got a sign that it's God's will.
Now everytime when I wish to really sleep
I go back to my secret retreat
back to the place where I dwelled...
before this World happened to me!

35. The Callings

Callings keeps calling...
I wonder why?
They pull you towards them
and that bizzare feeling suddenly ends.
Does it happen only to me?
Nah, it will happen to you eventually.
Callings keeps calling
till you merge in them.

36. I need you

In arguments you become rude,
ruthless and brute
these are the adjectives that define you so perfectly.
It's such a dichotomy,
You are the one I hate and love the most.
Isn't it an uncanny situation,
where I wanna runaway from you
and at the same time spend every breath and the rest of my life with you.
I get perplexed,
seeing myself in a unsettling mess, I stop, I stare
and I think about all the goodtimes and badtimes that we have sailed through.
I weigh them and try to measure the intensity
of the havoc you have created for my fragile being
but every time I do that, your love weighs more
and I am left with the realisation that
"I NEED YOU" more than ever before!

37. Not anymore

I no longer intend to be in your good books
because I have realised that you are not good
at reading in-between the lines.
I no longer want to be a good girl
because I have realised it's nothing
but a beautiful trap.
I just want to be honest to my core and
be the best that I can,
not to please anyone but to justify my being.
I leave it upto you to decide,
according to your set parameters
in which category I fall in.
I will accept it with full grace
with a solace in my heart that I'm no longer
deceiving myself anymore.

38. Misfit

Am I a traveller who happened to
be thrown back onto the timeline from the future
to make amends for my past mistakes…
or some blast from the past
whose impatience unwilling to stride along with the time
rushed ahead to see the future!
Sometimes I feel I'm a misfit in this perfect place...
though I can vouch for that that be it any era
I will always be the perfect fit for the missing
piece of your heart.

39. It's all mutual

The butterfly cannot fly,
without the wings..
The player is futile,
without the game.
The leader is incomplete,
without the followers!
The benefactor is nothing,
without beneficiary.
The Creator and the creation
are equally important..
their purpose is pointless without each other .
Relativity is the key to all of the existence..
Nothing exists in isolation... it all mutual!

40. Rare treasure

There are some old souls residing on the Earth
briming with unconditional love in their hearts.
They are relentlessly working towards their goal.
Comforting each soul with their selfless mission,
to heal the World!
Spreading joy, bringing smile to every face,
they are not in millions but very rare.
They carry a subtle spark that glows in the dark.
Treasure troves they are of a kind kind heart.
Blessed are those whose paths they cross.
And if you ever feel their presence just soak in
their divine essence...
For when the World gets through with the churn,
you will be one with them.
These rare jewels are sacred,
keep them close
they will ever warm the cockles of your heart.

41. Unconditional love

Sometimes I think, "Unconditional love" is that even a thing?
It's only to flaunt in front of all, nothing beyond.
Everyone is hungry to encash
without a mishmash for their personal benefit.
Checked every corner, knocked every door
couldn't sight one example to quote!
Then I thought, "What about mother's love, isn't that unconditional?"
Well yes to a great extent, parents do love their
children seldom asking for anything in return,
but still some expectations do cling.
So who is it that dares to love unconditionally?
I found an answer in a tree leaf!
It's only nature that gives unconditionally
without any prejudice without any claim.
The Sun, The Moon, The Rain and The Earth
they just selflessly keep giving to every being without
keeping an account, unbothered how grateful is the receiver
and never asking anything in return.
There's immense power in unconditional love
I wonder how many of us can really dare to do so.

42. Promise

I might look bad in someone's story
but I always want to look the best
in our love story.
The apparent freckles and flaws in me
scare me to come face to face with you.
You may not find me worthy of your love,
but I just want to tell you that
I have dared to bare my spotless soul
and loved you with all my heart.
You may fully accept or disown me but
I promise to become my best
if not in this...
some another lifetime!

43. Daily dose

Just like the food I eat and water I drink
Just like the thoughts I chase and dreams I see
You are a part of my essential routine
the much needed daily dose for my being.

44. The door

You were the one who closed all doors
I kept knocking, screaming at the top my voice.
You were the one who locked me up
I kept knocking with breathless sighs.
You were the one burning bridges to my heart
I kept knocking and let out a silent cry.
In that moment is when I realised...
You were the one who left crack in the the wall
for me to get hope and break it up.
You were the one who stirred up my soul
gave me strength to perserve through struggles.
You were the one who gave me wings to fly
everytime you saw me giving one more try.

45. Fine line

It appears surreal
but is absolutely clear.
A fine line marks
the fake from real!
Zircon from Diamond
Twenty two from pure gold
Artificial from authentic
Bought, from sold!
Plastic from organic
Immature from evolved!
It's apparant in many subtle ways,
just cannot be missed
A fine line is always there!

46. In control

I'm in the driving seat
but you are the driver...
I'm in the battlefield
but you are the warrior...
I'm taking the charge
but you are the Incharge...
Nothing seems to be in control
yet I am trusting you with my soul.

47. Solidarity

I stand in solidarity with,
my dream.
I stand in solidarity with,
my truth.
I stand in solidarity,
with my being.

48. Not my Home

I carry the Sun in my heart
and
Moon within my soul...
Earth is my workplace
and
not my home...

49. Just like me

The Universe says, "Your wish is my command"
and...
does everything that it feels like doing,
just like me!

50. S and S Combinations

Shorts and Spaghetti
Sugar and Spice
Smart and Sexy
Stop and Surrender
Serve and Support
Soul and Spirit
Sparkle and Shine
Sun and Stars
Shiv and Shakti

51. Stay silent

You made me quiet,
to find a way to reach you
For sure in my silence
I will find a way to reach you.
Now you stay happy in your silence
but deep within my heart,
I know that this silence
will also make you reach me.

52. World beyond

Religion, Politics and Relatives
are highly combustible topics
for any kind of discussion!
I'm done and dusted with
these kind of petty arguments.
I want to evolve and make a resolve,
though it will be little difficult
for me to remove the cloured glass
and cross these rigid line.
But once I do that, then everything's
gonna be just fine.
My love, hold my hand,
let's cross these mental barriers and for once,
and try to believe in each other's disbelief.
Isn't it high time?
Let's explore the beautiful World together.

53. It's complicated

It's simple yet complicated
playing the game called, "Life"
Wishing to win the game we get carried away
It always hurts the way circumstances put us
like opponents across a chessboard.
Checkmate is my aim to win the game
but you corner me in a stalemate time and again.
I don't like to loose yet I love to see you win.
We stretch the game and portray
as if we are perfect strangers.
We might be very good actors
but in our hearts there's an inbuilt lier detector.
We are both friends and foes
our equation often gets complicated
but thanks to our love that keeps it simple.
Now before you wake up and we end up in
another battlefield,
I better hug you and sleep by your side
with a victorious smile on my face.

54. Negotiation

I preserved and nurtured myself,
for you my love.
After years of waiting,
finally my prayers were answered.
I wholeheartedly gifted myself to you,
perhaps I came too easy to you
so you took me as any other play.
I know I am not mistaken...
it's just that you are not yet awakened.
You have played enough
with my love and emotions.
Now come let's sit across the table
and crack a fair deal to heal...
for apart from life and death
ain't everything negotiable?

55. I am not sorry

Musk isn't sorry,
for it's seductive smell
Pearl isn't sorry,
for being in the shell.
Sun isn't sorry,
for shinning so bright.
Moon isn't sorry,
for hiding at night.
Sky isn't sorry,
for being so blue.
so am I,
NOT sorry
for loving YOU...

56. Power hug

A genuine heartfelt hug feels like,
as if you have plugged into Nirvana.
It works like a miracle drug.
It's hangover lasting a lifetime...
perhaps even more!
Lucky are those who have acceces to its
luxurious warmth!
Rendering you totally satiated...
no matter how anxious one maybe
a power hug can make you calm!

57. The wheel

Often heard from the most authentic and reliable sources
that the wheel of Dharma rotates
if you follow the path of truth.
Keeping an eye on it but
haven't really seen it move an inch off late.
It's a conflict no longer between human beings
but of truth and malice.
So I have taken upon this challenge
to leave no stone unturned
and walk the difficult path with ease.
Because this time I am willing
to patiently wait and witness
the eternal play
and see the wheel spin
just the way you spun my World!

58. Unmask

Beneath the Cloak,
there's a Light which looks familiar...
Inside the Garb,
there's a Soul which works as elixir...
Even if you choose to stay in the mask,
there's a truth which is naked and clear!

59. It's good

It's good to be insane
in this sane world.
It keeps you going without a tumble...
It's good to be imperfect
in this perfectionist world.
It keeps you quite humble...
It's good to be insecure
in this seemingly sure world.
It keeps you sane & alive in this jumble!

60. Be like

Be like the radiance in my skin
let the world know it's all deep within.
Be like a smile on my face
let the world know it's all your grace.
Be like the best version of mine
let the world know it's all divine.
Be like a shine in my life
let the world know now there is no strife.

61. In it

In the cosmic net,
but not caught up...
In the material soup,
but not drowning...
In the worldly muck,
but not dirty...

62. Share space

In between the land and the sky
with you I want to share some space
that in my fantasy world is the safest place.
A place we have together visited a thousand million times
and rejuvinated our love
in numerous lifetimes.
Across the valley in my dreams, where the yellow flower beds lay
My sacred hub reflects in the river on every fullmoon night,
reminiscing patiently to have us in it's arms again.

63. Holy shit

I don't like you
for the holy shit you create.
But I love you
for the holy shift that always permeates.

64. Fair deal

Get me the Moon my love
and
I will share my Sunshine with you.
Get my smile back my love
and
I will share all my joys with you.

65. On hold

Can't handle life's congestion
hence stopped all interjections.
Now I seek your protection,
to become merely your projection.
Only with your guided direction,
I will take any further action.

66. Inked

The tattoos on my body
are visible ink marks.
But my soul is permanently
inked with your love!
Wish you could see through...
the invisible layers of my heart.

67. Warriors

Everyone is busy fighting their own battles,
but some... are fighting for a higher cause!
Though soldiers come bound to an authority,
Warriors are beyond any measures and boundries.

68. My favourite

Unintentionally you have become...
my favorite distraction.
Unknowingly you have become
my most treasured possession.
Undoubtedly you have become
my most reliable motivation.
Unquestionably you are the one
always providing the solution.
I hope and pray,
you continue to keep my faith in you
for our timeless connection.

69. Fuel it

Haters increase the intensity of your hatered,
need to fuel the fire...
And the ones who love please love me a liitle more
for you are such a blissful shower...
The unrest is not out of hate or love either
it's just my unquenched desire,
that needs to be placed on pyre.

70. Innocent child

I see a child in you
who needs to be entertained all the time.
What do you expect me to do?
I can dance, I can sing, I can do whatever you want me to
but I just want to remind you
that somewhere...
there's an innocent child inside me too!

71. Between you and me

Between you and me is a distance as long as infinity.
Between you and me are milestones without certainity.
Between you and me are impediments with surety.
Between you and me feelings defy the rules of gravity.
Between you and me the essense draws clarity.
Between you and me is a bittersweet reality.
Between you and me exists a paradox of rationality.
Between you and me yet remains only purity.

72. Long drive

Can we just go for a long drive
long enough to make this life feel short...
Can we just go for a long drive
good enough to create memories to my heart's delight.
Can we just go for a long drive
smooth enough to rest my head on your shoulder and sleep.

73. Assumption

You assumed me to be your student
when I don't even remember,
signing up for the course!
Making me learn lesson after lesson
without even asking,
if I want to know more!
Though I indulged you for a while,
you took the liberty
to test me to your heart's delight!
O life, here I am...
enrolling for the rest of the your course,
let me be at peace without troubles anymore!

74. Open heart

All I can offer you is my open heart.
Trust me it's full of love and warmth.
It's upto you, to break it or take it.
Whatever maybe your choice,
I promise to keep offering the same
time and again, for that's my aim!
To Love you...
with everybeat of my heart!

75. Sometimes

Sometimes it's not about perfection,
but just reflection.
Sometimes it's not about conception,
but just deception.
But in deception... there always is perfection!

76. Thank you

When I became weak,
you gave me strength.
When I lost my vision,
you showed me hope.
When I lost my foundation,
you carried me in your arms.
When the spell was tough,
you gave me the wand to transcend.
Thank you Almighty
for always being there for me.

77. Redirected to You

In happy moments my heart
redirects me to you in gratitude.
In angry moments my mind
redirects me to you in quandary.
In exhilarating moments my body
redirects me to you in ecstasy.
In sad moments my soul
redirects me to you in surrender.
In triumphant moments my spirit
redirects me to you in grace.

78. Interrogation

In the process of emptying myself of me,
am I filling myself with you?
Nah! I cannot...
What I am, is already you!
I am just going through the process
of rediscovering you within me.

79. Come back

Show some benevolence, don't leave me alone
for I'm not a stranger but your very own.
What do you think, I could have taken away,
when all that I needed was pure love!
You took the cue to escape
when all that I asked from you was to stay.
So wish you could simply come back,
just the way you walked away.

80. Blueprint

Some say, the road is spiral
but there's no authentic blueprint.
Some say it's difficult to cross the rabbit hole,
but there's no assured way to find.
Some say there is a chasm between me and you
but there's no joining bridge.
But my Heart says follow the fireflies within
to walk the path that connects straight to your heart.

81. Journey

Mundane chapters to thrilling phases,
all lived as destined by fate...
Sometimes crawling at snail's pace
sometimes rushing through the gate...
Spring, summer, autumn or winter
I never flinched though you tried to intimidate!
On the way met some souls who remained pauper,
no matter how high they put up their rate!
Crossed paths with few others
who selflessly chose to share their light.
Such has been the journey of my life!

82. One sided relationship

Our relationship dynamics keep changing.
When I assume that you are watching my back
I find you standing right amongst my opponents.
Doubts creep in when you betray my trust!
They say, long distance relationships don't last for long
but I still want to give it another try.
I gather the scatered pieces of my heart
and try to regain my faith in you with a hope,
that you will support me the next time.
Alas! Again I see you putting hurdles on my way.
There's definitely something amiss...
or is it some kind of a mirage that I have got enamored with?
I feel betrayed in this one sided relationship!
Tell me, do you really love me
or is it some kind of spritual sedative
that I'm put on!

83. Fantasy

Life will always be full of imperfections
fantasies can be the way you want it to be.
No gate crash, no road rash,
only our beautiful love stash!
No allegations, no blame games, no expectations
what a lovely place it would be
with only you and me.
Where love would no more be a fantasy
but an indescribable reality.

84. Free ride

How much does it take,
to earn one free ride
to the blue mountain and the word so far?
How much does it take,
to deserve one free ride
to the full Moon and the twinkling Stars!
How much does it take,
to claim one free ride
to settle forever in your beating heart?

85. Address

Do you still use some ancient bandwidth!
Neither is there high speed network,
nor any app's to communicate...
Please share your live location, landmark,
email ID, address...
Some contact detail!
Your agents don't deliver the message anymore...
My mom and dad must be waiting eagerly!
I know that they are there with you,
I am worried they might be stuck up in some stampede!
The GPS trackers fail to trace you.
Don't know how to communicate anymore...
Please speak up and lead me to your place.

86. If only

No words, no poetry, no prose would ever justify
my emotions roiling within!
If only,
you could read my eyes,
you would feel my soul waiting high and dry.
If only,
You could hear my silence
you would understand, the pain in my heart.
If only,
You could feel my breath
You would realise, the depth of my love.

87. Inspired

Running behind the squirrels,
chasing the colourful butterflies,
plucking flowers to make garlands and
waiting for the ripened fruit to fall off from the tree...
these are my cherished childhood memories.
Time flew by with some sweet lies and some bitter truths.
The clock kept ticking and so did my heart...
skipping a beat or two for a long while.
Life was slipping away without an anchor to hold on to!
Then out of the blue you came,
just like a fresh breeze...
picture perfect in every frame of my life's reel.
Ah! I thank God that you transpired
and with you in it, my life became inspired.

88. Found it

In pain I found pleasure,
In distress I found peace,
In chaos I found order,
In defeat I found victory,
What a deceptive game of Life!

89. Break open

Just like the foetus in the mother's womb
that need to come out for its life to bloom
I'm immensely grateful to all those...
who broke my loving heart.
It dialated in a way for my light to pass through
givng me courage to walk alone through the
darkest tunnel without any support!
I am so thankful to all those
who cut me up in different parts...
for it has freed my soul
to heal as many broken but loving hearts!

90. Thought

You are the first thought when I wake up.
You are the one I surrender to before I sleep.
I don't do it consciously...
I rather try to abstain myself from this pleasure
and when I do that I profusely breathe!
So to ease the pain I allow your thought
to be with me again...
Leaving no room for seperation...
I'm one with you again!

91. Empty

Some chapters, will always remain empty
as I'm without you.
Because nothing can be
written in these chapters,
they are complete in our incompleteness.
Such is the destiny of these chapters
they are helplessly tied to their fate...
Just like us!

92. Make me happy

It doesn't take much to make me happy!
I am not hungry for a mouthful of sky,
but just for someone to sing me a lullaby.
I am not hungry for a thousand accolades,
but just for someone I could chitter-chatter till late.
I am not hungry for millions to make me shine,
but just for a bunch of good souls who I can call mine.
I am not hungry for followers across the globe,
but just for a loving heart who can give me hope.
Does it really take much, to make me happy?

93. Resonate

I'm not a "touch me not plant"
but to be handled with care kind of a person.
I refrain from creating any ruckus
to gain your attention or become the center of attraction.
But yes, I do long for your affection and undivided attention.
My delicate being, resonates...
by the way you pluck the the strings within me!
Every cord exudes affection when touched with love
and agony when you try to tame me!
I'm quite sensitive to your indifferent cruelity!
Approach me with some genuine warmth...
and I assure to resonate as your favourite melody.

94. Bewitched

Don't want to come out of this spell
Don't want this beautiful trance to end
Don't want this illusionary bubble to break
Am I in a bewitched state!?
And then I think...
What if it's the other way round?

95. Simply

The child in me just wants to claim the whole World!
Wants to laugh and live life whole heartedly.
Challenges keep forcing her to grow up
but the naughty child always
finds a way to rescue her innocence.
She is adamant to enjoy the game
in spite of being told that the rules have changed.
She is passionate about every small and
big things she does in a day.
The clock keep ticking and she is told,
"no more are you a child, so better play your age."
She pleads to seek some more time
wishing to give her best shot.
Time and again she wants to claim the whole World!
But within she knows that nothing belongs to her!

96. What's your name?

By the way what's your name?
Time and again you get acclaim!
Each one has a unique tale to proclaim.
What's your claim to fame?
I realise there's no time no fixed frame
you are as much in small and big flame
By the way what's your name?
Master, do tell me else I stop playing the game!

97. Look at me now

Look what have you done to me...
should I laugh or should I cry?
Should I feel satisfied and celebrate...
that no matter what happened
I always gave it a try and
didn't let the life just pass by!

98. No dues

As a rule I don't ask for anything from anyone
except you!
But off late, I have dropped the idea
and stopped doing that too...
Somewhere I know you will prove
that I haven't paid my due...
Can you just keep all those things aside
for once without a review?
Please sit by my side with a smile,
without making me wait in the queue.
We will enjoy watching the starlit sky
and smell the flowers covered with dew!
Can we take a pause and feel each other...
for such timeless moments in life are few!

99. No guts No glory

The way you made me transcend my limitations
has rendered me totally in awe of your being!
Got strength to tread like a seasoned one on the difficult path,
when I thought I would tumble and fall!
Maybe that's why they say, "no guts no glory"
though I have realised without goof-ups...
there is no story!
Ah! Indeed I have committed blunders ...
that cannot be pardoned.
Don't know how many lifetimes will be required
to cull the latent darkness and lit up the fire!

100. Spectator

Actions speak louder than words,
but your actions are contradictory!
You choose silence over words...
watch everything like a moot spectator
and yet want my trust to be unshaken.
I hate your confidence in me...
no matter how weak or strong might be my resolve,
You trust that I will do it!

101. You Know what

You know what...
just fool the Wizard and be with me!
You know what...
just fabricate the World and look at me
You know what...
just forget the Worries and dream with me
You Know what...
just fuse the wishes and love me...

102. On a friendly note

In awe of the abundance all over the earth!
In every species, be it plant, animal or humans that disperse
there is plenty of beings of all kinds...
To be honest,
quantity overshadows the quality
there's genuine dearth of virtue and purity...
Please don't be offended,
please don't inflame.
I remember very vividly that I'm just a small fry.
I took the liberty to bring to your notice
on just a friendly note.

103. Apology

I have a propensity of being passionate about
everything I do.
All through my life I had a vague image in my mind
of the one who I would love with my passionate heart.
The picture kept forming over the years...
bit by bit adding definition and color,
eliminating my fears.
It would act absolutely according to my whims and fancies!
Absolutely perfect just like my dream...
you came into my life and reigned supreme.
We shared the joys with zest but the difference
between my dream and reality was...
the way you responded was
not as per my set standards of your role.
What bugs me immensly is that,
you have vitiated my flawless perception of you.
I feel you owe me an apology or perhaps...
I need to apologise myself for having such a dogmatic mindset!
Somebody surely needs to apologise so that I
can passionately continue to love you
and live my life happily ever after!

104. All yours

So I have decided to give away everything
that belongs to you...
I want to hand over everything to you
that's yours, including me.

105. Waves

Waves have no fixed pattern or intensity
just like my feelings and thoughts...
Sometimes I surmount acute high tides
sometimes fall down even when the tide is low!
Unpredictablility of these ups and downs make me anxious
I'm trying hard to be centered in my core...
so that joys and sorrows won't spoil my play!

106. What the poet wants to say!

What does the poet want to say?
Wonder if anyone ever,
truly grasped the intention of the poet when she pens a thought!
Wish, somebody could feel the soul of her words...
just like tenderness and jagged edges between lovers.
The poet innocently pours lots more than what she wants to say,
like a Cuckoo who doesn't want to die with the song in her heart.

107. Hide and seek

I have had your fleeting glimpse
here and there but then you disappear.
Why do you hide,
when all you want from me is to seek!
So many times I get cornered
rules of the game none bothers to share!
If that's what you want then so it be
just stop playing dirty with me!
In my longing to meet you
trying everything I can...
Concede, surrender, bow down to your plan!

108. Realign

When everything seems intertwined
but you don't need to unwind...
know you are smitten by the divine!
It time to shun ego, just realign...
feel the melody of silence and see core shine!

About Unsent Letters

In the month of June 2020, amidst the chaos that reigned supreme due to the unprecedented pandemic, when everyone was fighting their own battles exacerbated by the lockdowns. It was becoming hard to share one's feelings and fears, that's when I discovered a way to express myself.

Emotionally overwhelmed, with reasoning blurred shattered longings and unanswered questions swirling in mind, in that moment I surrendered yet never gave up. Trusting the divine, I allowed myself to soak all up and synthesize, which gave birth to, " UNSENT LETTERS".

Unsent letters is a collection of some soul- stirring conversations, some unshared perspectives, some taboo talks, some grievances and most of all lots of love straight from the heart. It gave wings to my imagination to connect to the one's who got disconnected either by fate or by distance.

On this journey I discovered my true self and it made me fell liberated. It's a humble attempt with the little knowledge that I have gained and wisdom that has been acquired to bring forth a heartfelt tribute to all those who have been as vulnerable as me.

I have a hunch that *Unsent Letters* will navigate its way through the matrix of time, and its spirit will get delivered to all those who need it indeed.

About The Author

Prache was born in Jaipur (Rajasthan), brought up in Ambala (Haryana), married in Amritsar (Punjab) and finally settled in Mumbai (Maharashtra). Her maternal grandfather -Nanna ji- was a notable freedom fighter and paternal grandfather -Bauji- was a prominent businessman. In a big joint Arya Samaji family, her mother followed Sanatan Dharam; she did her schooling from an Orthodox Convent School and eventually got married to a Sikh! Perhaps being exposed to different religions up close from the very onset, to seek divine became an integral part of her being.

Unfortunately she lost the core pillar of her life, her Mother when she was just 18 and then her Father. The void that they left behind made her see life from a different perspective.

Though life was always full of adventure for her -she participated in Maruti Suzuki Women's Drive Car Rally & Gladrags Mrs. India Contest- but adventure took a different turn when she married Manpreet Arshi, an awarded Screenwriter and actor's Director. Sometime in-between she also had two near death experiences which made her a firmly believer in living each moment of life to its fullest.

After completing her Masters in Commerce from Kurukshetra University she qualified U. G .C (N.E.T) and started her carrer as a College Lecturer. Nurturing her creative side she did a Scriptwriting course conducted under the aegis of National Film Development Corporation in association with Netflix. She is a screenwriter of a short film, “Pep Talks” which got released on Pocket films' Digital platforms in September 2021. She has also authored a Novel, "Second Chance", published in January 2022.

Her quest to know and learn more about life and divinity has always kept her on toes. Spiritual teachings and their application in her routine life has made her keep abreast with the incessant callings of her soul. With all the twist and turns that life has put her though she believes in having a heart to heart connect with her audience and readers and touch those subjects that are insightful and relatable for them.

Printed by Libri Plureos GmbH in Hamburg,
Germany